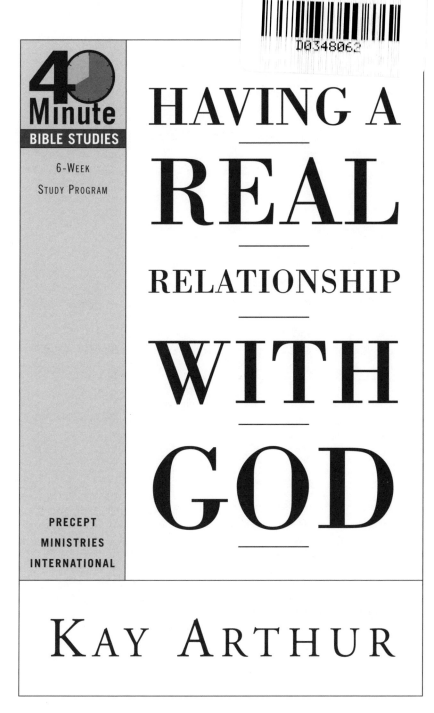

40 Minute

BIBLE STUDIES

6-WEEK
STUDY PROGRAM

PRECEPT
MINISTRIES
INTERNATIONAL

HAVING A
REAL
RELATIONSHIP
WITH
GOD

KAY ARTHUR

HAVING A REAL RELATIONSHIP WITH GOD
PUBLISHED BY WATERBROOK PRESS
2375 Telstar Drive, Suite 160
Colorado Springs, Colorado 80920
A division of Random House, Inc.

ISBN 1-57856-477-8

Printed in the United States of America
2002

10 9 8 7 6 5

HOW TO USE THIS STUDY

This small-group study is for people who are interested in learning more about what the Bible says, but who have only limited time to meet together. It's ideal, for example, for a lunch group at work, an early morning men's group, a young mother's group meeting in a home, or a smaller Sunday-school class. (It's also ideal for small groups that typically have longer meeting times—such as evening groups or Saturday morning groups—but want to devote only a portion of their time together to actual study, while reserving the rest for prayer, fellowship, or other activities.)

This book is designed so that all the group's participants will complete each lesson's study activities *at the same time, while you're together.*

However, you'll need a facilitator to lead the group—someone to keep the discussion moving. (This person's function is *not* that of a lecturer or teacher. However, when this book is used in a Sunday-school class or similar setting, the teacher may want to lead more directly and to bring in other insights in addition to those provided in each week's lesson.)

If *you* are your group's facilitator, the leader, here are some helpful points for making your job easier:

- Go through the lesson and mark the text before you lead the group. This will give you increased familiarity with the material and will enable you to facilitate the group with greater ease. It may be easier for you to lead the group through the instructions for marking if you use colored pencils to color-code the words you mark.

- As you lead the group, start at the beginning of the text and simply read it aloud in the order it appears in the lesson, including the "insight boxes," which may appear either before or after the instructions or in the midst of your observations or discussion. Work through the lesson together, observing and discussing what you learn. As you read the Scripture verses, have the group say aloud the word they are marking in the text.

• The discussion questions are there simply to help you cover the material. As the class moves into the discussion, many times you will find that they will cover the questions on their own. Remember the discussion questions are there to guide the group through the topic, not to squelch discussion.

• Remember how important it is for people to verbalize their answers and discoveries. This greatly strengthens their personal understanding of each week's lesson. Try to ensure that everyone has plenty of opportunity to contribute to each week's discussions.

• Keep the discussion moving. This may mean spending more time on some parts of the study than on others. If necessary, you should feel free to spread out a lesson over more than one session. However, remember that you don't want to slow the pace too much. It's much better to leave everyone "wanting more" than to have people dropping out because of declining interest.

• If the validity or accuracy of some of the answers seems questionable, you can gently and cheerfully remind the group to stay focused on the truth of the Scriptures. Your object is to learn what the Bible says, not to engage in human philosophy. Really *read* the Scriptures, asking God to show everyone His answers.

HAVING A REAL RELATIONSHIP WITH GOD

Have you ever wondered if it's possible to have a meaningful relationship with God? An authentic relationship that works in the day-in-and-day-out circumstances of life? Do you hunger for a genuine experience of community and of God?

This is an inductive study that will help you discover for yourself how such a relationship is possible. By *inductive* we mean you are going to go straight to the source—the Bible—to see what God has to say about the relationship He wants to have with you and about the community He wants to bring you into.

Leader: Take a few minutes and discuss where our culture is and what people are seeking. What are some of the questions they are asking? How do they feel about life? about God? Do they have a religion that works? a belief—a relationship—that has changed their lives? One that they feel is authentic?

OBSERVE

Have you ever wondered what we have to do, what we have to become in order to merit a relationship with God? Let's read what God has to say in the New Testament book of Romans.

Leader: Read aloud Romans 5:6-11. Have the students circle the words **we** *and* **us** *in the text. As the students mark each pronoun, have them say it aloud as you come to it in the text. That way everyone will be sure to mark every reference.*

Ask the students to read through the same verses again on their own, and when they come to the word **love,** *to mark it by drawing a heart over it, like this:* ♡

ROMANS 5:6-11

6 For while we were still helpless, at the right time Christ died for the ungodly.

7 For one will hardly die for a righteous man; though perhaps for the good man someone would dare even to die.

8 But God demonstrates His own love toward us, in that while we were yet sinners, Christ died for us.

9 Much more then, having now been justified by His blood, we shall be saved from the wrath of God through Him.

10 For if while we were enemies we were reconciled to God through the death of His Son, much more, having been reconciled, we shall be saved by His life.

11 And not only this, but we also exult in God through our Lord Jesus Christ, through whom we have now received the reconciliation.

INSIGHT

Sinners means people who basically run their own lives, doing things their own way rather than God's way. Therefore they fall short of God's standard and separate themselves from God.

DISCUSS

According to verse 8, when did God demonstrate His love to us and how?

What was our status when God demonstrated His love to us?

Look at the occurrences of the words *we* and *us* that you have marked and discuss what you learn about the state of mankind when Christ died for them.

Does this raise these questions in your mind:

Why are we helpless?

What is a sinner?

Whose enemy are we and why?

Those are good questions that will be answered next week.

OBSERVE

Now let's take a closer look at this passage and see what these verses tell us about God and Jesus Christ.

Read through the text again on pages 6-7, each one on your own, and mark every reference to **God** and to **Jesus Christ.**

Mark God like this: △

Mark Jesus Christ with a cross: †

ROMANS 5:6-11

⁶ For while we were still helpless, at the right time Christ died for the ungodly.

⁷ For one will hardly die for a righteous man; though perhaps for the good man someone would dare even to die.

⁸ But God demonstrates His own love toward us, in that while we were yet sinners, Christ died for us.

⁹ Much more then, having now been justified by His blood, we shall be saved from the wrath of God through Him.

¹⁰ For if while we were enemies we were reconciled to God

List everything you have learned about God and about Jesus Christ in the sidebar column on page 7.

INSIGHT

Justified means to be acquitted, to be declared not guilty, to be made righteous, to be put in right standing.

Reconciled means to no longer be at enmity (or enemies) with one another. The dictionary definition is "to make friends again; to win over; to settle a quarrel, a disagreement; to make satisfied; to be no longer opposed."

Reconciliation means to change from being at enmity (or separated) to becoming friends.

DISCUSS

What did you learn about God from these verses?

What did you learn about Jesus Christ from these verses?

In whose eyes do we need to be justified? Why?

How are we are justified?

According to verse 9, what do we need to be saved from? How will we be saved? What does this tell you about people who never have an authentic relationship with God?

through the death of His Son, much more, having been reconciled, we shall be saved by His life.

11 And not only this, but we also exult in God through our Lord Jesus Christ, through whom we have now received the reconciliation.

GOD

JESUS CHRIST

Discuss what it means to be reconciled so you make sure you understand what you read in the Insight Box. Then discuss how and when we are reconciled to God. What did Christ do that made that reconciliation possible? (You may have covered this already, but review is good—so go for it!)

INSIGHT

We didn't become sinners at enmity with God because God pulled away from mankind, abandoning us, leaving us on our own. Our relationship with God was damaged by man's own willfulness. At the beginning of creation, Adam and Eve, the first man and woman God created, made a choice to listen to someone else rather than to God. Like rebellious children, they walked away from the protection of being obedient to their Creator and Sustainer. Adam's decision to eat something God had forbidden him to eat broke his intimacy with God. Consequently we became ungodly sinners, enemies of God.

WRAP IT UP

Just think: If we are reconciled by Jesus' death on the cross, then verse 10 of Romans 5 says we shall be saved by His life! In other words, Jesus didn't stay dead. He rose from the dead. He lives and we will live too, saved by His life. We will look at this in greater depth later.

The question you need to ask yourself is this: Where do you stand in your relationship with God if the Bible is true? Are you a sinner, ungodly, and an enemy of God? According to what you have read, is there hope for you? Can you have an authentic relationship with God?

Have you received reconciliation and become God's friend—or does there seem to be something standing in your way? If it's the latter, do not despair. There is hope. Simply talk to God about it. Tell Him where you think you are and what your questions are. Then wait for Him to answer. He will, because He longs to have an intimate and meaningful relationship with you!

Next week we're going to take a good look at this issue of sin. What makes us sinners in God's eyes? What is sin? What form does it take, and where does it lead? It will be most enlightening.

In an age when many in our society lack integrity…when our ethics and actions rest completely on our personal judgment, feelings, desires, and opinions…when the buzz word is *tolerance*…and absolutes are rejected—we need to know how God defines sin and what sin leads to.

Leader: *Take a few minutes and have the students discuss the morals and ethical standards and beliefs of those with whom they associate at church or socially. What are their perceptions of Christianity and the position of the church on various social and moral issues?*

OBSERVE

Now let's find out how God describes sin.

Leader: *Read aloud the verses in the sidebar columns of pages 11-13, beginning with 1 John 3:4 and finishing with Isaiah 53:6. Have the students put a circle with a slash through it at every occurrence of the word* **sin,** *like this:* ⊘ *Also mark the word* **iniquity** *in the same way. Again, have the students say the word out loud each time you come to it.*

1 John 3:4

Everyone who practices sin also practices lawlessness; and sin is lawlessness.

1 John 5:17

All unrighteousness is sin, and there is a sin not leading to death.

James 4:17

Therefore, to one who knows the right thing to do and does not do it, to him it is sin.

ROMANS 14:23

But he who doubts is condemned if he eats, because his eating is not from faith; and whatever is not from faith is sin.

JOHN 16:7-9

7 "But I tell you the truth, it is to your advantage that I go away; for if I do not go away, the Helper will not come to you; but if I go, I will send Him to you.

8 "And He, when He comes, will convict the world concerning sin and righteousness and judgment;

9 concerning sin, because they do not believe in Me."

DISCUSS

Go through the Scripture verses one by one and discuss how each defines sin. As you do, see if someone can give an example or illustration that clarifies that specific definition of sin.

Leader: Read aloud the definitions for "lawlessness" and "unrighteousness."

INSIGHT

Lawlessness is breaking or ignoring God's laws; living apart from God's laws.

Unrighteousness is living contrary to what God says is right.

Based on these definitions, who should we look to in order to find out what is "right" and what is "not right"? What, according to these verses, do we call that which is "not right"?

Faith is taking God at His Word, believing what He says is true. If you say you believe God, according to Romans 14:23, how then will you live? If you are going to live by faith, what is necessary for you to know?

The words in John 16:7-9 were spoken by Jesus Christ. The pronoun *He* in verse 8 refers to the Holy Spirit. What does the Holy Spirit do?

According to Isaiah 53:6 what have the sheep done wrong? Have you ever done that? Is anyone brave enough to share when he or she willfully chose to walk in a way contrary to what was right? What was the end result?

Based on what we have learned about unrighteousness and lawlessness, what does it mean that we have gone our own way? What is that called?

ISAIAH 53:6

All of us like sheep have gone astray, each of us has turned to his own way; but the LORD has caused the iniquity of us all to fall on Him.

INSIGHT

Iniquity is a synonym for lawlessness, unrighteousness, sin.

According to Isaiah 53:6, what has God done with "the iniquities of us all"? Does that remind you of anything you learned last week?

ROMANS 3:9-10

⁹ What then? Are we better than they? Not at all; for we have already charged that both Jews and Greeks are all under sin;

¹⁰ as it is written, "There is none righteous, not even one."

ROMANS 3:23

For all have sinned and fall short of the glory of God.

OBSERVE

*Leader: Read aloud the verses in the sidebar columns on pages 14-16 and have them mark **sin** as they did previously. (Don't forget to also mark the word **iniquity** the same way.) Again, have the students say the word aloud each time you come to it.*

The book of Romans is a letter written by the apostle Paul to a group of Christians in Rome. When Paul used the pronoun *we,* he included himself and his companions among those who were once helpless, ungodly sinners and enemies of God.

DISCUSS

What do you observe about the extent of sin from the passages in Romans?

In Romans 5:12, do you know who the "one man" is through whom sin entered into the world? If not, read the last Insight Box in Week One. If, as the Bible says, all humanity descended from one man, then what is inherent in man? What verse in the sidebar column shows that to be true?

What did sin bring with it? And how widespread is sin? According to this passage, what entered the world because of sin? Has death spread to all men? What then does this show us about all men?

According to Psalm 51:5, in what condition does the psalmist say he was conceived? What does this say about every child born into this world?

Who then, according to these verses, can claim to be without sin? Do you see yourself as a sinner? Why or why not?

ROMANS 5:12

Therefore, just as through one man sin entered into the world, and death through sin, and so death spread to all men, because all sinned.

PSALM 51:5

Behold, I was brought forth in iniquity, and in sin my mother conceived me.

JOHN 8:30-36

30 As He spoke these things, many came to believe in Him.

31 So Jesus was saying to those Jews who had believed Him, "If you continue in My word, then you are truly disciples of Mine;

32 and you will know the truth, and the truth will make you free."

33 They answered Him, "We are Abraham's descendants and have never yet been enslaved to anyone; how is it that You say, 'You will become free'?"

34 Jesus answered them, "Truly, truly, I say to you, everyone who commits sin is the slave of sin.

35 "The slave does not remain in the house forever; the son does remain forever.

36 "So if the Son makes you free, you will be free indeed."

In John 8:30-36, what does Jesus say is true about the one who commits sin? Do you see the truth of this verse manifested in society today? How?

Also according to John 8:30-36, who is the only one who can set the slave "free indeed"?

If, as Jesus says in John 8:32, "truth will make you free," where is truth to be found?

WRAP IT UP

We have seen that the Bible says all men have sinned. So what does this mean to us and our relationship with God? Are there serious consequences to sin? Will a righteous God excuse our behavior if we blame it on our upbringing, our parents' failures, our place in society, or our environment? Can we deny that we are sinners and hope to reach heaven? Next week we will look at what the Bible tells us of the consequences of sin.

We have seen that, according to the Word of God, all people are sinners and are slaves to sin. We are born that way and will remain that way until Jesus Christ sets us free.

We have also gained a biblical understanding of what constitutes sin. The question that now needs to be considered is this: According to God, what are the consequences of sin? Or, if I don't believe in God, should I even care?

OBSERVE

Leader: Read aloud John 8:18-24. Also read verse 44, which appears on page 21. Jesus is speaking to the Pharisees, the Jewish religious leaders of His time, as He stands in the temple treasury on the Temple Mount (the current site of the Dome of the Rock in Jerusalem). Have the group mark:

- *every reference to **sin** or **sins,** like this:*
- *every reference to **the Jews** (including the pronouns **they, them,** and **you**) with a **J.***
- *every reference to **Jesus** with a cross:* †

JOHN 8:18-24

18 "I am He who testifies about Myself, and the Father who sent Me testifies about Me."

19 So they were saying to Him, "Where is Your Father?" Jesus answered, "You know neither Me nor My Father; if you knew Me, you would know My Father also."

20 These words He spoke in the treasury, as He taught in the temple; and no one seized Him, because His hour had not yet come.

21 Then He said again to them, "I go away, and you will seek Me, and will die in your sin; where I am going, you cannot come."

22 So the Jews were saying, "Surely He will not kill Himself, will He, since He says, 'Where I am going, you cannot come'?"

23 And He was saying to them, "You are from below, I am from above; you are of this world, I am not of this world.

INSIGHT

In John 8:24, the word *He* was added by the translators. When Jesus says they must believe that He is "I Am," He is making reference to the name God uses for Himself in the Old Testament book of Exodus. This is the name God gave Moses when Moses asked Him His name at the burning bush. God's response was, "I Am…. This is My name forever, and this is My memorial name to all generations." In other words, Jesus is telling the Jews that He is God, one with the Father.

DISCUSS

What did you learn about Jesus Christ from this passage?

What did you learn about the Jews/Pharisees?

What do the Pharisees have to believe in order not to die in their sins? If that is true for them, do you think it would be true for you as well?

OBSERVE

Leader: Read the Scripture passages in the sidebar columns on pages 21-24, starting with Numbers 32:23. As before, those in the group should mark the word **sin** *and any reference to* **those who commit sin.** *Also have them mark any* **synonyms for sin.**

Make sure the group says "sin" aloud each time you come to it or its synonyms.

DISCUSS

What does Numbers 32:23 say about sin?

24 "Therefore I said to you that you will die in your sins; for unless you believe that I am He, you will die in your sins...."

JOHN 8:44

"You are of your father the devil, and you want to do the desires of your father. He was a murderer from the beginning, and does not stand in the truth because there is no truth in him. Whenever he speaks a lie, he speaks from his own nature, for he is a liar and the father of lies."

NUMBERS 32:23

But if you will not do so, behold, you have sinned against the LORD, and be sure your sin will find you out.

1 CORINTHIANS 6:9-11

9 Or do you not know that the unrighteous will not inherit the kingdom of God? Do not be deceived; neither fornicators, nor idolaters, nor adulterers, nor effeminate, nor homosexuals,

10 nor thieves, nor the covetous, nor drunkards, nor revilers, nor swindlers, will inherit the kingdom of God.

11 Such were some of you; but you were washed, but you were sanctified, but you were justified in the name of the Lord Jesus Christ and in the Spirit of our God.

Have you ever tried to hide something you did that you know you should not have done? What would God call what you have done? From what we see in this verse, do you think anyone can hide their sin from God?

What synonym(s) for sin do you see in Galatians 5:19-21?

What specific sins are listed in 1 Corinthians 6:9-11, Galatians 5:19-21, and Revelation 21:8? You may want to underline each of the sins to make sure you don't miss any.

INSIGHT

Carousing—drunken parties.

Dissentions—to be divided from one another.

Effeminate—not only males but any person who is guilty of addiction to sexual sins; a person who allows himself to be sexually abused contrary to nature. Would include cross-dressing.

Emulations—jealousy, envy.

Enmity—hatred, to be an enemy.

Faction—taking sides.

Fornicator—a person who engages in illicit sexual intercourse. Includes adultery, incest, bestiality, pornography.

Revilers—abusive speech.

Sensuality—uncontrolled lust, lacking self-control.

Sorcery/Witchcraft—use of drugs for nonmedical purposes or for magical purposes.

GALATIANS 5:19-21

19 Now the deeds of the flesh are evident, which are: immorality, impurity, sensuality,

20 idolatry, sorcery, enmities, strife, jealousy, outbursts of anger, disputes, dissentions, factions,

21 envying, drunkenness, carousing, and things like these, of which I forewarn you, just as I have forewarned you, that those who practice such things will not inherit the kingdom of God.

REVELATION 21:8

But for the cowardly and unbelieving and abominable and murderers and immoral persons and sorcerers and idolaters and all liars, their part will be in the lake that burns with fire and brimstone, which is the second death.

REVELATION 20:14

Then death and Hades were thrown into the lake of fire. This is the second death, the lake of fire.

ROMANS 6:23

For the wages of sin is death, but the free gift of God is eternal life in Christ Jesus our Lord.

Leader: Discuss these sins using the definitions in the Insight Box on page 23 to help clarify their meanings.

Do you see any of these sins in the world today? How? Where? Are they called "sin" by the world's definition?

What consequences do you see for sin in these passages?

What contrast do you see in 1 Corinthians 6:11? How did this change occur? Review the meaning of the word *justified*. (It was discussed in Week One.) Do you see that there is a hope for those who are "slaves to sin"?

According to Revelation 20:14, what is the "second death"?

What does Romans 6:23 describe as being the "wages" or payment for sin?

What kind of death do you think this verse is referring to? Could it be merely physical death? Note the contrast with sin and what we have already seen about the consequences for sin in the previous verses. Also go back to Week One and look again at Romans 5:9. Do you think there's any relationship between the "wrath of God" and the lake of fire, the second death?

Leader: *Challenge the students to stop and consider what would happen to them if they died today. Where would they be? The Bible tells us that it is appointed for man to die once, and then comes the judgment (Hebrews 9:27).*

WRAP IT UP

What have you learned about sin in your life and how it affects your relationship with God? What will happen to you should you die in your sins? Do you think God is serious about sin and its consequences?

The next time you hear a comedian joke about the things God deems sin, just remember that sin is serious, with eternal consequences. According to God, it can keep you from ever experiencing life.

But, friend, there is hope. There is help! A way has been prepared for you and me to be right with God and to be accepted by God. God has made a way for us to get rid of the enmity that sin creates. Reconciliation is possible if you come to God on His terms. That is good news that we will look at next week.

WEEK FOUR

Last week we learned about sin. We saw where sin came from, who is guilty of sin, and what the penalty for sin is. It is a rather grim and frightening reality to know that all have sinned and that the penalty for sin is death. But if you are wondering if there is a light at the end of the tunnel, there is! God is a faithful and loving God, forgiving and offering hope to all who will believe the good news. It's the good news of the gospel that brings you into a meaningful relationship with God!

You do not have to be a slave to sin. You can be reconciled to God.

This week we are going to see what the gospel is and how it can set us free from the bondage and penalty of sin.

OBSERVE

First Corinthians is another letter written by the apostle Paul, in this case his first letter to the church at Corinth. The culture and morals in Corinth were much like those of today.

*Leader: Read through 1 Corinthians 15:1-10 and have the group mark every occurrence of the word **gospel** with a megaphone like this:* ⊏▭▭◗ *Also have them mark all its synonyms and the words **which** and **what**, if they refer to the gospel. Have the group say "gospel" aloud as you come to it.*

1 CORINTHIANS 15:1-10

1 Now I make known to you, brethren, the gospel which I preached to you, which also you received, in which also you stand,

2 by which also you are saved, if you hold fast the word which I preached to you, unless you believed in vain.

3 For I delivered to you as of first importance what I also received, that Christ died for our sins according to the Scriptures,

4 and that He was buried, and that He was raised on the third day according to the Scriptures,

5 and that He appeared to Cephas, then to the twelve.

6 After that He appeared to more than five hundred brethren at one time, most of whom remain until now, but some have fallen asleep;

7 then He appeared to James, then to all the apostles;

*Leader: Now have the students read through the text again. This time have the group circle every reference to the **Corinthians** (to whom Paul is writing) and mark every reference to **Jesus Christ,** including all the pronouns, with a cross.*

DISCUSS

What do you learn in verses 1-2 from marking all the references to the Corinthians and to the gospel?

In verses 3-4, Paul outlines the gospel message. What was the message of the gospel that Paul delivered?

What are its main points?

As you read verses 3-4, did you notice the repeated phrase? Mark this phrase in a distinctive way.

What two things happened "according to the Scriptures"?

According to verses 4-9, what events took place that proved that these two things actually occurred?

INSIGHT

When the text says "according to the Scriptures," Paul is referring to the Old Testament, because at the time he wrote 1 Corinthians, the New Testament portion of the Bible was not yet complete. So God is letting us know that these truths, these points of the gospel, are contained in the Old Testament.

8 and last of all, as to one untimely born, He appeared to me also.

9 For I am the least of the apostles, and not fit to be called an apostle, because I persecuted the church of God.

10 But by the grace of God I am what I am, and His grace toward me did not prove vain; but I labored even more than all of them, yet not I, but the grace of God with me.

Last week, when we looked at Romans 6:23, what did you learn about sin?

The author of Romans contrasts this payment for sin with the free gift of God in Christ Jesus. According to the gospel, who paid for your sins? How was the debt paid?

2 CORINTHIANS 5:14-21

14 For the love of Christ controls us, having concluded this, that one died for all, therefore all died;

15 and He died for all, so that they who live might no longer live for themselves, but for Him who died and rose again on their behalf.

OBSERVE

Let's look at another passage in order to understand better what Jesus' death and resurrection accomplished for you and me.

*Leader: Read aloud 2 Corinthians 5:14-21 and have the group mark every reference to **Christ** and the pronouns referring to Him. Make sure to have them say "Jesus" aloud each time you come to a word that refers to Him.*

*Also circle every occurrence of the words **we** and **us**.*

DISCUSS

One of the most efficient ways to find out what a passage is talking about is to interrogate the text using the "five *W*s and an *H*"—who, what, when, where, why, and how. Interrogate this passage to learn all you can about Jesus Christ.

What did Christ do, according to this passage?

Who did He do it for?

Why did Jesus become sin on our behalf, according to verse 21?

What did you learn from marking the words *we* and *us*?

Do you think this can pertain to you?

16 Therefore from now on we recognize no one according to the flesh; even though we have known Christ according to the flesh, yet now we know Him in this way no longer.

17 Therefore if anyone is in Christ, he is a new creature; the old things passed away; behold, new things have come.

18 Now all these things are from God, who reconciled us to Himself through Christ and gave us the ministry of reconciliation,

19 namely, that God was in Christ reconciling the world to Himself, not counting their trespasses against them, and He has committed to us the word of reconciliation.

20 Therefore, we are ambassadors for Christ, as though God were making an appeal through us; we beg you on behalf of Christ, be reconciled to God.

21 He made Him who knew no sin to be sin on our behalf, so that we might become the righteousness of God in Him.

According to verse 17, what changes happen when we are in Christ?

INSIGHT

In Christ—This term is used to describe the status or state of a person who has believed the good news and taken it to heart, embracing the good news (the gospel) personally.

OBSERVE

You have probably noticed a repeated key word as you observed this passage: the word *reconciled,* along with its other forms, *reconciling* and *reconciliation.* It's a word you saw in our study in Week One when we looked at Romans 5. Remember that this term means to change from being at enmity (enemies), or separated, to becoming friends. It denotes a change in relationship.

Leader: Have the students mark reconciliation like this ⋈ as you read through 2 Corinthians 5:14-21 once more.

DISCUSS

What did you learn from marking these references to reconciliation? Answer as many of the five *W*s and an *H* that you can from the text, such as: Who was reconciled to whom? Who initiated it? How was it done? What was the result?

Cover the subject thoroughly. It will be a blessing and a challenge, for you must also note what the Christian's role is in reconciliation.

After studying sin and the penalty of sin, why is it important that God not count our trespasses against us?

What is the "ministry of reconciliation"? (Look at what Paul's ministry was in verse 20.)

Why do you think there would be such an urgency to tell others to be reconciled to God? Do you find this difficult to do?

If so, you are not alone. If you have time, discuss this as a group. Learn from one another how to overcome your reticence.

WRAP IT UP

Now then, what are you going to do with the knowledge you have gained these past four weeks? Will you take God at His Word and believe Him? Are you willing to have a genuine change of mind (the Bible calls that "repentance") regarding your thoughts about God and about yourself? Do you believe you are a sinner? Will you in faith take God at His Word and believe that Jesus' death paid for all your sins?

When a person genuinely repents, this change of mind brings a change in behavior. You will no longer walk as "sheep [who] have gone astray" and as someone who keeps turning "to his own way" (Isaiah 53:6). Once you are willing to repent, you need to believe that God means what He says. Tell God you will receive Jesus Christ as your Lord and your Savior. When you do this, my friend, God saves you from the penalty of your sins and gives you the ability to be saved from the power of sin itself.

If this is your desire, tell God that you want Him to set you free from your slavery to sin. You cannot free yourself, but God can free you—and He will, if you only ask. Thank God for sending His Son—the Lord Jesus Christ, God in the flesh—to die for your sins. Thank Him for raising Jesus Christ from the dead, and tell Him you want to walk in the newness of life that Jesus won for you through His death, burial, and resurrection.

Now then, if you are already a genuine Christian, are you living like a new creature? Or are you still carrying the burden of your past? Is what you did in the past—and what you were in the past—keeping you from walking in the freedom of His forgiveness? If so, you need to remember what you have just learned: "From now on we recognize no one according to the flesh" (2 Corinthians 5:16)—you are a brand-new creature! Old things have passed away and all things have become new. Now, beloved of God, live accordingly.

Authentic relationships are based on knowledge—on truth. Therefore it is important for you to understand how the penalty for your sins can be paid in full.

From last week's study we know that Jesus Christ died for our sins. He was made sin for us and died in our place. But who was Jesus that He could pay for our sins? How do we know His death resulted in paying the penalty for our sins? Let's look at several passages that tell us who Jesus was and why He was able to die as our substitute.

In order to be our substitute, Jesus had to be without sin. If He were born in sin or if He committed sin, He would have had to die for His own sins, because the wages of sin is death.

OBSERVE

*Leader: Read aloud Romans 5:12 and Matthew 1:18-23, reprinted in the sidebar columns; once again have the group mark every reference to **Jesus Christ** and any pronouns and synonyms that refer to Him (for example, **child** and **son**).*

DISCUSS

According to Romans 5:12 how did death spread to all men? Through whom did it spread?

ROMANS 5:12

Therefore, just as through one man sin entered into the world, and death through sin, and so death spread to all men, because all sinned.

MATTHEW 1:18-23

18 Now the birth of Jesus Christ was as follows: when His mother Mary had been betrothed to Joseph, before they

came together she was found to be with child by the Holy Spirit.

19 And Joseph her husband, being a righteous man and not wanting to disgrace her, planned to send her away secretly.

20 But when he had considered this, behold, an angel of the Lord appeared to him in a dream, saying, "Joseph, son of David, do not be afraid to take Mary as your wife; for the Child who has been conceived in her is of the Holy Spirit.

21 "She will bear a Son; and you shall call His name Jesus, for He will save His people from their sins."

According to Matthew 1:18-20, how did Mary conceive or get pregnant with Jesus?

Would Jesus have sin within Him? Was He born of man, the sperm of a man? Who was the father of Jesus Christ?

What will Jesus do, according to Matthew 1:21? Could He do that if He were a sinner?

OBSERVE

Leader: Read aloud Hebrews 2:14-15 and have the students mark **Christ** *as they did in the earlier passages.*

DISCUSS

According to Hebrews 2:14-15, what are the two reasons Jesus became a man—a human being made of flesh and blood?

Based on our previous study, who is in slavery? Why is there a fear of death? What makes death so dreadful? Isn't it what awaits us if our sins are not paid for in full?

Sin gives Satan his power, but if our sins are taken care of, then Satan has no power over us! Awesome!

22 Now all this took place to fulfill what was spoken by the Lord through the prophet:

23 "Behold, the virgin shall be with child and shall bear a Son, and they shall call His name Immanuel," which translated means, "God with us."

HEBREWS 2:14-15

14 Therefore, since the children share in flesh and blood, He Himself likewise also partook of the same, that through death He might render powerless him who had the power of death, that is, the devil,

15 and might free those who through fear of death were subject to slavery all their lives.

HEBREWS 10:4-10

4 For it is impossible for the blood of bulls and goats to take away sins.

5 Therefore, when He comes into the world, He says, "Sacrifice and offering You have not desired, but a body You have prepared for Me;

6 In whole burnt offerings and sacrifices for sin You have taken no pleasure.

7 "Then I said, 'Behold, I have come (In the scroll of the book it is written of Me) to do Your will, O God.'"

OBSERVE

*Leader: Read Hebrews 10:4-10 and John 1:29. Once again have the group mark every pronoun that refers to **Jesus Christ** in these verses. For example, the "He" in verse 5 refers to Jesus. Also mark references to **sin**.*

INSIGHT

The Old Testament book of Leviticus tells us that without the shedding of blood there can be no remission (or taking away) of sin (Leviticus 17:11).

Until the death of Jesus Christ, animals were sacrificed and their blood was used to cover man's sin.

DISCUSS

What did you learn from Hebrews 10:4-10 about Jesus Christ and His reason for coming into the world? What did Jesus do that the animal sacrifices could not do? How did He do it?

To be sanctified means to be set apart for God. How are we sanctified?

What happens to animal sacrifices once Jesus Christ has come? Why?

How does the Hebrews passage fit with what John the Baptist said about Jesus?

8 After saying above, "Sacrifices and offerings and whole burnt offerings and sacrifices for sin You have not desired, nor have You taken pleasure in them" (which are offered according to the Law),

9 then He said, "Behold, I have come to do Your will." He takes away the first in order to establish the second.

10 By this will we have been sanctified through the offering of the body of Jesus Christ once for all.

JOHN 1:29

The next day he saw Jesus coming to him and said, "Behold, the Lamb of God who takes away the sin of the world!"

2 CORINTHIANS 5:21

He made Him who knew no sin to be sin on our behalf, so that we might become the righteousness of God in Him.

1 JOHN 2:2

And He Himself is the propitiation for our sins, and not for ours only, but also for those of the whole world.

ROMANS 4:25

He who was delivered over because of our transgressions, and was raised because of our justification.

OBSERVE

Leader: Read aloud the passages in the sidebar column on this page. Have the group mark **Christ,** and all pronouns referring to Him, with a cross, as before.

INSIGHT

Propitiation—satisfaction, such as paying off a debt.

Transgression—a going aside, an overstepping, breaking a law.

Justification—acquitted, to be declared not guilty.

DISCUSS

Read the Insight Box together, then discuss what you have learned about Jesus from these passages. Discuss them one by one, and note the benefits you receive if you truly believe on Jesus Christ and receive Him as your Lord and Savior.

Just to make sure you don't miss this wonderful truth, recall that 1 John 2:2 tells us that Jesus Himself is the "propitiation." What was the propitiation for? Who was it for?

Remember the definition of this word *propitiation*. Then recall Romans 6:23 and the debt, the wages, that needed to be paid. See if someone can quote this verse from memory ("For the wages of sin is death, but the free gift of God is eternal life in Christ Jesus our Lord"—Romans 6:23).

Understanding that death is the wage for sin, what debt did Jesus pay and how did He do it?

According to Romans 4:25, why was Jesus delivered over? Look at the definition for justification. Why was Jesus raised? Was our debt paid? What is the proof?

WRAP IT UP

The proof of our justification is the resurrection of Jesus Christ from the dead. Yet some say, "Jesus didn't rise from the dead any more than He was born of a virgin!" Yet if Jesus had a human father and was born an ordinary man as the rest of us, then we have no "lamb unblemished and spotless" (1 Peter 1:19) to make atonement for our sins.

The blood of bulls and goats cannot take away our sin, neither can the tainted blood of sinful man. A sinner cannot die for a sinner and win his redemption. The Virgin Birth is essential to our salvation, and you must come to grips with it if you are to have a meaningful relationship with God. You cannot have an authentic relationship with someone you don't believe. Therefore you must choose: Will you believe the Word of God or the reasoning and rationale of mortal man?

Jesus paid for your sins. He died in your place. However, according to the gospel, Jesus did not stay dead: "He was raised on the third day according to the Scriptures" (1 Corinthians 15:4). The resurrection of Jesus Christ is our proof and our guarantee that God's holiness and justice were totally satisfied by the death of His Son.

So then, what about those who do *not* believe in the Resurrection, who say there is no resurrection? If they are right, what would be true? Paul addresses this problem in 1 Corinthians 15:12-19. Let's examine it, because understanding it is crucial to having a meaningful relationship with God.

OBSERVE

*Leader: Read aloud 1 Corinthians 15:12-19 and have the group mark each reference to Jesus Christ's **resurrection** ↑ (or lack of it ✗). Mark each reference to **Christ** with a cross.*

DISCUSS

Leader: Have the group move through these verses one by one and number all the things that would be true if Jesus Christ had not been raised from the dead.

1 CORINTHIANS 15:12-19

12 Now if Christ is preached, that He has been raised from the dead, how do some among you say that there is no resurrection of the dead?

13 But if there is no resurrection of the dead, not even Christ has been raised;

14 and if Christ has not been raised, then

our preaching is vain, your faith also is vain.

15 Moreover we are even found to be false witnesses of God, because we testified against God that He raised Christ, whom He did not raise, if in fact the dead are not raised.

16 For if the dead are not raised, not even Christ has been raised;

17 and if Christ has not been raised, your faith is worthless; you are still in your sins.

18 Then those also who have fallen asleep in Christ have perished.

19 If we have hoped in Christ in this life only, we are of all men most to be pitied.

If Jesus were not raised from the dead, where are you in your sins? And what about those who have died before you? What has happened to them?

According to verse 19, if Jesus was not raised, why would we—of all people—be most pitiable?

OBSERVE

*Leader: Read aloud John 11:25-26 and have the students mark the word **resurrection** like this ↑ as before.*

DISCUSS

According to these verses, how does Jesus describe Himself?

What is our guarantee if we believe on Him?

If, however, Jesus didn't rise from the dead after promising to do so, what does that make Jesus Christ?

Review the main points of the gospel and the evidence of those events that you studied in 1 Corinthians 15:1-10. Was there proof that Christ was raised from the dead? What was it?

JOHN 11:25-26

25 Jesus said to her, "I am the resurrection and the life; he who believes in Me will live even if he dies,

26 and everyone who lives and believes in Me will never die. Do you believe this?"

ROMANS 10:1-13

1 Brethren, my heart's desire and my prayer to God for them is for their salvation.

2 For I testify about them that they have a zeal for God, but not in accordance with knowledge.

3 For not knowing about God's righteousness and seeking to establish their own, they did not subject themselves to the righteousness of God.

4 For Christ is the end of the law for righteousness to everyone who believes.

You have examined God's Word. You saw that the Bible teaches that Jesus rose from the dead, and therefore there is a resurrection from the dead for all who are in Christ. Now then, are you going to believe the Bible or mortal man? You have God's Word. You know the gospel; what will you do with it?

OBSERVE

Leader: Read aloud Romans 10:1-13. Have the students put a big R over every reference to righteousness. Also mark every reference to Jesus Christ.

INSIGHT

The word *Lord* in this passage means "supreme in authority, master."

Righteousness is the opposite of lawlessness; it is "conformity to all that He commands or appoints."

DISCUSS

Leader: *Have the group identify the two kinds of righteousness contrasted in Romans 10:1-6.*

Two Kinds of Righteouness:

Righteousness of

_____

Righteousness of

_____

Which kind of righteousness are most people trying to have? What are some of the things they do to get it? What about you?

5 For Moses writes that the man who practices the righteousness which is based on law shall live by that righteousness.

6 But the righteousness based on faith speaks as follows: "Do not say in your heart, 'Who will ascend into heaven?' (that is, to bring Christ down),

7 or 'Who will descend into the abyss?' (that is, to bring Christ up from the dead)."

8 But what does it say? "The word is near you, in your mouth and in your heart"— that is, the word of faith which we are preaching,

9 that if you confess with your mouth Jesus as Lord, and believe in your heart that God raised Him from the dead, you will be saved;

10 for with the heart a person believes, resulting in righteousness, and with the mouth he confesses, resulting in salvation.

11 For the Scripture says, "Whoever believes in Him will not be disappointed."

12 For there is no distinction between Jew and Greek; for the same Lord is Lord of all, abounding in riches for all who call on Him;

13 for "Whoever will call on the name of the LORD will be saved."

According to all you have studied, has Jesus Christ already come down to earth? Has He already been brought up from the dead?

OBSERVE

Leader: Read Ephesians 2:8-9 aloud. "Grace" is unmerited, unearned favor with God.

DISCUSS

How does Ephesians 2:8-9 parallel what is said in Romans 10?

According to Romans 10, what must a person do to be saved? What must they believe? What must they confess?

What will such belief and confession save you from? (Think of all you have studied these past weeks, beginning with Romans 5:9 in Week One.)

EPHESIANS 2:8-9

8 For by grace you have been saved through faith; and that not of yourselves, it is the gift of God;

9 not as a result of works, so that no one may boast.

If Jesus is Lord—if He is God—what should He have authority over in your life?

Are you ready to give Him total control? If not, why not? In the light of all that God and Jesus Christ have done on your behalf, don't you think you can trust God as your Father and trust Jesus as your Lord?

Jesus trusted God to raise Him from the dead. You can trust Jesus to do the same— He is the resurrection and the life. Do you believe that?

WRAP IT UP

If Jesus had not been raised, there would be no justification for our sins, and we, of all people, are most to be pitied because we're going to die in our sins. However, Jesus claimed that He was the resurrection and the life, and many witnesses saw Him after His death. In Jesus' own words, the question is asked: "Do you believe this?" If you do, you will live even if you die, and everyone who lives and believes in Him will never die (John 11:26). In other words, you will never experience the second death, because you have passed from death to life by believing in the Lord Jesus Christ. You have an authentic relationship with God, your forever Father. And you belong to His forever family. That's community!

Now then, how are you going to know what God "commands or appoints" so that you can conform to it? Well, the Bible is what God has given us so we will know how He wants us to live. You need to study it and know what it says so you can live as a true believer!

Precept Ministries International exists for that purpose, and we have a variety of ways to help you learn how to study God's Word for yourself and to grow more and more into His likeness. Just give us a call at 1-800-763-8280 or write us at P.O. Box 182218, Chattanooga, TN 37422.

This unique Bible study series from Kay Arthur and the teaching team of Precept Ministries International tackles the issues with which inquiring minds wrestle—in short, easy-to-grasp lessons ideal for small-group settings. These first five study courses in the series can be followed in any order. Here is one possible sequence:

How Do You Know God's Your Father?
by Kay Arthur, David and BJ Lawson
This six-week study looks at the change that takes place when a mortal human encounters a holy God. It focuses on John—who went from being a "son of thunder" to being "the disciple Jesus loved." The student will walk through the book of 1 John, taking note of the characteristics of a child of God versus those of a child of the devil.

Having a Real Relationship with God
by Kay Arthur
For those who yearn to know God and relate to Him in meaningful ways, Kay Arthur opens the Bible to show the way to salvation. With a straightforward examination of vital Bible passages, this enlightening study focuses on where we stand with God, how our sin keeps us from knowing Him, and how Christ bridged the chasm between humans and their Lord.

Being a Disciple: Counting the Real Cost
by Kay Arthur, Tom and Jane Hart
Jesus calls His followers to be disciples. And discipleship comes with a cost, a commitment. This study takes an inductive look at how the

Bible describes a disciple, sets forth the marks of a follower of Christ, and invites students to accept the challenge and then enjoy the blessings of discipleship.

How Do You Walk the Walk You Talk?
by Kay Arthur

This thorough, inductive study of Ephesians 4 and 5 is designed to help students see for themselves what God says about the lifestyle of a true believer in Jesus Christ. The study will equip them to live in a manner worthy of their calling, with the ultimate goal of developing a daily walk with God marked by maturity, Christlikeness, and peace.

Living a Life of True Worship
by Kay Arthur, Bob and Diane Vereen

Worship is one of Christianity's most misunderstood topics. This study explores what the Bible says about worship—what it is, when it happens, where it takes place. Is it based on your emotions? Is it something that only happens on Sunday in church? Does it impact how you serve? This study offers fresh, biblical answers.

THE "LORD" SERIES

While the 40-Minute Bible Studies are ideal for small-group settings where time is limited, the "Lord" series is designed to involve readers in the incomparably enriching experience of daily study in God's Word. Each book has been thoroughly tested and has already had an impact on a multitude of lives.

Lord, Give Me a Heart for You, the newest Lord study, examines the anatomy of a heart for God through the eyes of the apostle Paul. Throughout his ministry Paul was criticized, opposed, and attacked. He struggled with fragile relationships and was often weary, tired, and discouraged. You may have times when you identify with what Paul experienced. Yet you, like Paul, long to be a person whose sole passion is to please God. In this eight-week study you'll discover what a heart for God looks like when lived out in flesh and blood in the daily circumstances of life. As you study 2 Corinthians, Acts, and other portions of Scripture, you'll begin to understand what it's like to have a heart like His.

Lord, I Want to Know You is a foundational study for the "Lord" books. In this seventeen-week study you'll discover how God's character is revealed through His names, such as Creator, Healer, Protector, Provider, and many more. Within the names of God you'll encounter strength for your worst trials, comfort for your heart's deepest pain, and provision for your soul's greatest need. As you come to know Him more fully—the power of His glorious name and the depth of His infinite love—your walk with God will be transformed and your faith will be increased.

Lord, Heal My Hurts is, understandably, one of the most popular studies in this series. If you're in touch with the world, you know that people around you are in great pain. We run to many sources for relief when we are in pain. Some of us turn to other people; many escape into drugs, work, further education, and even hobbies. But in God you can find salvation from any situation, from any hurt. In this thirteen-week study you'll see that, no matter what you've done or what's been done to you, God wants to become your refuge…He loves you and desires your wholeness…and He offers healing for your deepest wounds.

Lord, I Need Grace to Make It Today will reveal to you in fresh power the amazing truth that God's grace is available for *every* situation, no matter how difficult, no matter how terrible. You'll gain the confidence that God will use you for His glory, as His grace enables you to persevere regardless of your need, regardless of your circumstances, and despite the backward pull of your flesh. You will see and know that the Lord and His all-sufficient grace will always be with you.

Lord, I'm Torn Between Two Masters opens your understanding to the kind of life that is truly pleasing to God. If you've known discouragement because you felt you could never measure up to God's standards or if you've ever felt unbearably stretched by the clash of life's priorities, this nine-week study of the Sermon on the Mount will lead you into a new freedom that will truly clear your vision and fortify your heart. You'll be encouraged to entwine your thoughts, hopes, dreams, and desires around heavenly things, and you'll find your life transformed by choosing to seek first God's kingdom and His righteousness.

Lord, Only You Can Change Me is an eight-week devotional study on character that draws especially on the so-called Beatitudes of Matthew 5. If you've ever been frustrated at not being all you wanted to be for the Lord or at not being able to change, you'll find in this study of Christ's teaching the path to true inner transformation that is accomplished only through the work of the indwelling Holy Spirit. You will learn the achievable reality of a godly life and the fulfillment it can bring.

Lord, Where Are You When Bad Things Happen? is a critically important study in preparing you for times of trial. In this ten-week course you'll be grounded in the knowledge and confidence of God's sovereignty as you study especially the book of Habakkuk and see how God works in and through difficult and demanding situations. More than that, you'll learn what it means to live by faith…and to rest the details of your life in His hands.

Lord, Is It Warfare? Teach Me to Stand is a study that trains you for spiritual battle. God's Word tells us that our adversary, the devil, goes about like a roaring lion seeking whom he may devour (1 Peter 5:8, KJV). Many times we either don't recognize this enemy, or we're scared by his roar. We would like him to go away, but it's not that simple. In this eleven-week study you'll learn how to recognize Satan's tactics and how to be set free from bondage. As you focus your study especially on the book of Ephesians, you'll discover how to build an unshakable faith that makes victory yours for the taking. (This is the most challenging of the "Lord" books and requires an average of two to two and a half hours of weekly preparation to complete the assignments.)

ABOUT KAY ARTHUR AND PRECEPT MINISTRIES INTERNATIONAL

Kay Arthur, executive vice president and cofounder of Precept Ministries International, is known around the world as a Bible teacher, author, conference speaker, and host of national radio and television programs.

Kay and her husband, Jack, founded Precept Ministries in 1970 in Chattanooga, Tennessee. Started as a fledgling ministry for teens, Precept today is a worldwide outreach that establishes children, teens, and adults in God's Word, so that they can discover the Bible's truths for themselves. Precept inductive Bible studies are taught in all 50 states. The studies have been translated into 65 languages, reaching 118 countries.

Kay is the author of more than 120 books and inductive Bible study courses, with a total of over 5 million books in print. She is sought after by groups throughout the world as an inspiring Bible teacher and conference speaker. Kay is also well known globally through her daily and weekly television and radio programs.

Contact Precept Ministries International for more information about inductive Bible studies in your area.

Precept Ministries International
P.O. Box 182218
Chattanooga, TN 37422-7218
800-763-8280
www.precept.org